Arizona's Probate Guidebook for Consumers

Help for Arizonans in Probate: A Hand When It's Needed Most

Francisco P. Sirvent

Learn MORE about how

WE can help

YOU get your loved one's estate

squared away

480-418-1776

Call our office TODAY!

Make your appointment for your Discovery Hour

www.KeystoneLawFirm.com

Table of Contents

Before you read more, can you answer these questions...

How would you define the current "problem" that is causing you to contact our law firm?

_____

_____

_____

_____

If that problem were to be <u>totally solved</u> (however you define it), what would look different in your life?

_____

_____

_____

_____

How Probate Works in Arizona

Thank you for requesting our Keystone Law Firm Probate Guidebook. Probate is a word everyone has heard, but few understand. After someone dies, their estate lives on – at least until probate has been completed. We've all heard about cases that drag on for years while heirs fight about who gets what, all the while depleting the funds they hoped to inherit. Or about people who find out their loved one's estate was never probated when they try to sell real estate or pull funds from a financial account. Although probate may be a new thing to you, it's best to quickly find out how and when to start the probate process.

Before we get into the details about probate, here are four things you should know right away to do within the first 24 hours after a loved one has passed.

Four Things to Do within 24 Hours of a Loved One's Death:

1. Determine whether any of decedent's property needs to be safeguarded, such as valuable assets, motor vehicle, and vacant home or vacant rental house. Ask who has keys to vehicles and properties.

2. Ensure that cremation or funeral arrangements have been made. The funeral home will order Certificates of Death from the proper state bureau or department.

3. If the decedent's address is in the obituary or the phone book and depending on where the home is located, consider hiring security or off-duty police officer to watch the decedent's house while the family is at the funeral.

4. Do not list the day and month of birth in the obituary, due to a new form of identity theft.

Everything else can wait until you've spoken with an attorney.

What Does Probate Mean and How Do I Know I Need to Do it?

If your loved one has signed a Will and there are assets over $75,000 of personal property or $100,000 of real estate equity you probably need to start a probate proceeding.

As soon as possible after someone's death, find their Will and other estate planning documents. Hopefully, your loved one has had a frank discussion with you about their plans and where to find their documents.

The best thing you can do now is to contact a qualified probate attorney, one who knows Arizona law. Provide as much information as possible to your attorney so he or she can advise you how to proceed. After speaking with your attorney, you'll both know which assets require probate and which do not.

In Arizona, there are at least three types of probate proceeding:

- **Informal probate**—The estate is settled with very little action from the probate court.

- **Formal probate**—The court may hold several hearings while the estate is being settled.

- **Supervised probate**—The court more closely supervises the administration of the estate.

Your attorney will tell you which type of proceeding is needed, if any, and how to file paperwork with the probate court. After that, the amount of time spent in court depends on the type of probate needed. A personal representative or executor will be appointed. After the executor has completed all required duties, like finding heirs or paying creditors, the probate proceeding will be closed.

Discussing your plans with you family member, and making sure they know where your documents are located is a great first step. During your estate planning discussions with your attorney you'll learn how to set up your assets for quick transfer to beneficiaries instead of waiting for all the probate time lives to pass.

Encourage your family and friends to talk about their life care plans. They don't have to discuss every detail of their estates or give everyone a copy of their Wills, but at least let executors know where your important legal documents are located so they can quickly act after your incapacity or death.

How to Choose a Probate & Trust Attorney

This is all they do.

Like most things in life nowadays, you want to work with someone who is an expert. You know the old saying, "Jack of all trades, master of none." Some attorneys will handle DUIs, divorces, bankruptcies, wills & trusts, probates, and business matters. At Keystone Law Firm, we only do one thing: helping people plan & protect their estate matters.

Flat fees

We charge flat fees for most matters so you know what the cost is BEFORE you start and that you aren't going to get a $45 charge for a 5 minute phone call. There are a few certain types of cases that the probate court actually REQUIRES that we charge hourly. In those cases, we give you a **100% transparency promise** about expected costs and fees.

Defined process

Working with an attorney can be frustrating because the process is new to you. It is rare for law firms to have a published process of how they guide clients through projects and you can be left wondering, "What's the next step?" We have a clearly defined process with pre-scheduled appointments so you know what is going to happen next.

100% Satisfaction Guarantee

We give all of our clients a 100% Satisfaction Guarantee with our services. This is a red-flag if an attorney cannot figure out how to give you one.

Introduction to Probate

Probate is the process of transferring money or property <u>from</u> the name of a deceased person <u>to</u> the name of the rightful heirs. The local Superior Court probate division oversees the process.

You must go through probate if any of these things happen:

1. A bank, title company, lawyer, investment institution, insurance company, says you need:
   a. "Letters of Appointment"
   b. "Letters of Administration"
   c. "Letters of Executor"
   d. "Appointment as Personal Representative", or
   e. Anything similar to any of the above.
2. You want absolute certainty that all of the decedent's creditors are cut off from chasing after your inheritance.

Problem Spotter:

Lack of transparency is a very common complaint. Even if you are the authorized PR, you have a duty to be transparent.

3. Family members disagree about who should get what from the estate or who should be in charge of administering the estate.

4. While someone is still living, if they either did not have powers of attorney, or if others are not honoring their powers of attorney, or they are threatening to do themselves harm. (This is a reference to probate cases that occur during life: conservatorships & guardianships. This book is not going to discuss those issues. If you want to know more about them, contact our office.

There are three basic steps of probate administration: (1) collect, protect and manage the assets, (2) pay claims, taxes and costs of administration, and then (3) distribute estate assets.

Probate takes a long time

The fastest probate cases take *at least* six months. There is no getting around that. If there are any problems or delays along the way, an "easy" probate can take twelve months and a complicated probate case can take many years! So be prepared to tell everyone else involved that this is slow by design.

Difference Levels of Probate

1. Transfer by Small Estate Affidavit,

2. Summary Administration,

3. Informal Probate,

4. Formal Probate, and

5. Supervised Administration

Levels 1 through 3 are suitable when the money and property values are small, there is no challenge, and either an original Will exists or the family members all agree about who should be the court-appointed personal representative. Levels 4 and 5 provide additional layers of protection to the people involved in the probate case when necessary.

Levels 4 and 5 should only be attempted with the help of an attorney.

Phase 1:
Collecting & Protecting the Estate

Identifying Probate and Non-probate Assets

The first step in proceeding with administering any estate is to identify which assets (if any) need to go through probate. This process starts with establishing which assets are going to be subject to the probate court jurisdiction and which assets pass outside of the probate process. Every asset of the decedent will ultimately fall into one of these two categories. The most important step is to verify title! TITLE IS EVERYTHING when it comes to determining what is included in the probate estate.

Gather documents. For bank accounts, you will need the most recent bank statement; for real estate, the most recent deed; for life insurance, the most recent statement, policy, and beneficiary designations; etc. Only after each asset has a corresponding document to prove ownership and beneficiary designation, can you decide what goes through probate and what does not.

Probate Assets

Only those assets that are the decedent's separate property or his/her share of community property become part of the decedent's "probate estate".

Everything else is not part of the probate estate and is not subject to probate administration, except to the extent necessary to satisfy statutory allowances and creditors claims.

The deceased's person portion of jointly owned assets is included in the decedent's estate so long as the decedent's interest does not extinguish upon his/her death—like it does with rights of survivorship. If something was owned as "joint tenants", the deceased's person's share is a probate asset.

Non-probate Assets

Non-probate assets are any, typically, assets that are joint with right of survivorship, or those with TOD/POD or valid beneficiary designations.

Joint Assets

Joint assets come in two forms: with right of survivorship (ROS) and without. Joint assets that *do not have* rights of survivorship are probate assets. Whether the joint assets are community property with a spouse or tenants in common with a non-spouse, the result is the same: if the asset was not owned with ROS, the decedent's share must be included in his/her probate estate.

Bank Accounts

Multiple party bank accounts and pay-on-death (POD) designations qualify as non-probate assets. Upon the death of one owner in a multi-party bank account, the bank will pay the balance of the account to the survivor(s) only if the account carries with it a right of survivorship. If no ROS exists, the deceased party's interest in the account is a probate asset. When an account has a POD designation, the beneficiary takes the account balance after all surviving owners have deceased.

Life Insurance / Employee Retirement Plans

Life insurance and annuity proceeds are not typically part of the probate estate because they pass according to the terms of the insurance contract beneficiaries. The only exception to this is if the policy names the "estate" as the beneficiary or if the named beneficiary is also deceased.

The same is normally true for employee retirement plans (Roths, IRAs, 401ks, etc.). These accounts pass strictly according to the terms of their beneficiary designations to the named beneficiaries, or if none, to the beneficiaries as designated in the plan contract.

Real Estate

Real estate will be included in the probate estate unless it was owned with ROS, a beneficiary deed was recorded before the death, or in some form of trust.

Trusts and other immediate transfers on death

Trusts are widely used to completely avoid probate upon a person's death. Basically, the trust takes the asset out of an individual's name during his/her life and puts it in the name of the trustee (i.e., "John & Mary Smith, trustees of the John & Mary Smith Trust Agreement, dated 1/1/2009 and any amendments thereto") so that upon their death, the asset was not and is not owned in their individual name. The trust continues in existence after the death and the successor trustee begins to administer all of the trust assets in accordance with its terms. Similar arrangements can be made using limited liability companies, limited partnerships and other entities if asset protection or tax reduction is desirable.

Considerations for the Small Estate

Arizona's flexible probate system allows for some small estates to be administered *without any formal judicial oversight.* This subset of procedures provides a series of steps that can be used after various times have passed after the person's death; in some cases 5 days and in other cases 6 months.

Transfer by Small Estate Affidavit

Probate through the court system is not mandatory for small estates where the **total estate value** is below $75,000 (net of liens and encumbrances). The rightful successor(s) may claim entitlement and recover the small estate property by presenting the person in possession of the property with an affidavit. This can be used to gather money on deposit in a bank, stock certificates, vehicles, jewelry, money owed to a decedent, and investments, but it cannot be used to transfer real estate.

If the assessed value of **real estate** is below $100,000 (net of liens and encumbrances), the rightful successor(s) can prepare and file a real estate affidavit with the probate court, pay the probate court and recording fees, and, if approved, effect a valid transfer of the real estate to the successor(s).

Probate Estate Is not "Small Enough"

You must file a probate case if the estate assets are more than the limits set out above.

The PR is the person responsible for collecting and protecting the estate assets. The priority of who will be appointed as the PR is in this order:

6. Person nominated by will

7. Spouse who is also a devisee

8. Other devisees

9. Surviving spouse

10. Other heirs

11. Department of Veteran's Affairs

12. Any Creditor (at least 45 days after death)

13. Public fiduciary

If no person is nominated by will and there are more than one person(s) who share the same priority, the group must agree or present evidence on who will be nominated. Anyone who will be acting as a PR must go through the court training materials.

The three types you can file are called informal, formal, or supervised. Which type to file is a somewhat complicated and strategic decision, but in general you will file an informal probate case when you have an **original will** or **no will** at all. In all other cases, you will be filing a formal probate.

Filing Informal Probate

Prepare the following documents and have the applicant sign & notarize where necessary:

- Original Will,

- Application for Informal Probate and Appointment of Personal Representative,

- Statement of Informal Probate,

- Letters and Acceptance of Appointment,

- Order to Personal Representative,

- Notice of Application and Proof of Notice of Application, and

- (if applicable to your situation also have ready) Waiver of Right to Appointment and Waiver of Bond.

File with the probate registrar, pay the fee, and wait for the approval. Each county has different methods of informing you of the approval. Your approval will come with one document that is the magic piece of paper: "Letters of Appointment". It should be certified as an original by the court clerk. Keep these safe and don't give it away or let anyone remove the staple, as that will uncertify the document.

Once approved, send copies of the Notice of Appointment and Admission of Will to Probate, Statement of Informal Probate of Will and Appointment of Personal Representative and Order to PR to all "interested persons" within 10 days of the approval.

(Formal probate proceedings follow a similar path as the informal proceedings, but they require a court hearing before the PR can be appointed. If you think you need to file a formal probate, please call our office so we can plan out a good strategy for you. Formal probates should not be attempted without the help of a probate attorney.)

Problem Spotter:

Never mix estate money with your own. If you already did, you may have a problem.

Publish the Notice to Creditors (once a week for three consecutive weeks) and mail it to each known creditor of the estate. This will bar any creditors' claims after four months if they fail to file a claim.

The PR must now take possession of all estate property (remember, this is the "collect & protect" phase). This ensures that the PR can fulfill his/her duty to prevent waste of estate assets. It is not necessary to take possession of estate assets if (1) the PR determines that the asset is already in the possession of the person presumptively entitled to it and (2) the value will not diminish should a sale of the asset be needed at a later time to pay claims. If someone appears to be hiding estate assets, the PR can petition the court and force the person to testify regarding papers, documents, assets, property or other interests of the decedent.

The PR should take title to any probate estate assets in the following format:

"<<Personal Representative>>, the personal representative
of the estate of <<Decedent First Name/Last Name>>".

You can alternatively name it as

"the estate of <<Decedent First Name/Last Name>> by
<<Personal Representative>>, personal representative"

Money on deposit at financial institutions (checking, savings) can usually be transferred to the estate account by presenting a certified copy of the death certificate and a certified copy of the letters of appointment to the institution. Real estate transfers should be done by special warranty deed and recorded in the county where the property is located. Vehicles can be transferred from the decedent's name to the PR's, heir's or devisee's name. The PR will need all of the proper Department of Motor Vehicle forms and fees, plus a certified copy of the Order Appointing the Personal Representative, and a written release or permission from any lien holder allowing the change of ownership.

You need the following items to open an account at most banks:

- Certified Letters of Appointment and/or Order Appointing PR

- Certified death certificate

- Tax ID Number

- Opening deposit (optional)

Always have the PR open a new bank account to receive deposits, pay the decedent's claims, and pay any expenses of administration. Only withdraw money from the estate checking account by checks and debit card transactions; NO CASH WITHDRAWS.

The PR will need a tax ID number (TIN) for the estate before a bank will open the account. Go to www.irs.gov and request an employer ID number (EIN), which is the same thing as a TIN in this case. Or obtain form SS-4 and request the TIN by mail, fax or phone. If you request it online, you get the TIN at the end of the interview in a matter of minutes.

Before 90 days after appointed as PR, prepare and file the Inventory & Appraisement. This document must list property details, fair market value, its character as separate or community, and debts or liens against the property. The inventory may be filed with the court (which will make it a public record) or it may be mailed to all interested persons and a Proof of Mailing filed with the court. If the PR determines that the estate size is less than allowances and exempt property ($37,000), the Notice to Creditors is not required and the PR can close the estate by summary procedures.

Phase 2:
Handling Claims against the Estate

Now that the PR has a handle on what the assets of the estate are, the PR must begin to deal with any claims of the estate. Paying claims is one of the responsibilities and, if done incorrectly, can become personal obligations of the person acting as PR.

Priority of Allowances, Claims and Taxes

The PR owes a duty of a fairness and impartiality to all successors of the estate when preparing for distribution. *In re Estate of Fogleman*, 197 Ariz. 252, 3 P.3d 1172 (App. 2000); *In re Estate of Shano*, 177 Ariz. 550, 869 P.2d 1203 (App. 1993).

Claims of an estate should be paid in this order:

1. Costs and expenses of administration;

2. If there is a surviving spouse or minor children: Homestead allowance $18,000 (A.R.S. § 14-2402.B.) and exempt property ($7,000.00 A.R.S. § 14-2403.D.);

3. If there is a surviving spouse or minor children, the family allowance not to exceed $12,000 (A.R.S § 14-2404.B.);

4. Reasonable funeral expenses;

5. Debts and taxes with preference under federal law;

6. Reasonable and necessary medical and hospital expenses of the last illness of the decedent, including compensation of persons attending him;

7. Debts and taxes with preference under the laws of this state;

8. All other claims.

In estates where there is plenty of funds to pay all claims, the PR should pay the claims regardless of their priority and as soon as possible to avoid late fees and interest. Insolvent estates present more complex problems to determine which creditors will be paid. If the PR mistakenly pays the wrong claim, the PR is personally liable to the other creditor for the error.

Problem Spotter:

If you are the PR, pay off every bill before distributing money.

If you get this part wrong, you will owe the money.

Allowing/Disallowing Claims

The PR has the duty to not only notify known creditors of the probate proceeding, but also to review each creditor's claim and decide whether the claim is proper. The PR has 60 days *after* when the first Notice to Creditors was published in the newspaper to review and disallow claims. Any claims that are not disallowed are allowed. A claim can be disallowed by sending the creditor a Notice of Disallowance of Claim within the time permitted.

The PR should disallow any claim that was barred prior to the decedent's death due to the relevant statute of limitations. Any other claims that are not presented during the "time for presentation of claims" are completely and forever barred against the estate.

The PR has no authority to pay claims presented after this period without the consent of all affected parties.

Encumbered Assets

The PR can deal with assets in the estate that are encumbered by lien, mortgage, pledge or other security interest in two manners: (1) pay the encumbrance and take possession of the asset free of any claim, or (2) convey the asset to the creditor to satisfy the lien. In making this decision, the PR must decide what is in the best interest of the estate. Any deficiency that remains on the lien may become a claim against the estate, but the deficiency would fall into the lowest priority of claims under A.R.S. § 14-3805.

If the asset is given to an heir or beneficiary, the debt must still be paid and the heir's share is not automatically increased to offset.

Canceling Utilities and Credit Cards

If the decedent owned residential real estate where no surviving spouse or dependents are living, the PR should consider the cost of maintaining utilities until the house is sold or transferred to the heir/devisee and weigh that against simply shutting the utilities off. Some buyers won't look at a house unless they can verify that power and water sources are functioning.

Cable, phone and internet should be cancelled immediately after the death if they do not operate any of the utilities or alarm system.

If the decedent held any credit cards in his/her sole name, those companies will most likely automatically terminate the accounts upon receipt of the Notice to Creditors. But to ensure that the estate's identity is not stolen before that is sent, the PR should diligently contact each account by phone, notify them of the death, shred all credit cards and monitor each account for unauthorized activity. If any unauthorized activity occurs on the cards after the date of death and the PR has taken these steps, the estate will not be liable for those charges. Also have the PR check with each account to see if the decedent had paid for any form of credit insurance that pays his balance in the event of death. This benefit can be a gift to the residuary heirs and devisees.

Medical Insurance and Public Assistance Claims

In many cases, the decedent may have experienced a prolonged illness prior to his/her death and incurred significant medical expenses. Make sure to determine whether or not she had health insurance, either through Medicare, AHCCCS, employer or a private policy. Taking full advantage of these benefits can significantly decrease the burden of claims on the estate.

If the decedent was receiving ALTCS Medicaid benefits to pay for long term care expenses, the PR should research whether ALTCS has filed a lien against any property of the decedent. If an asset was "exempt" while the decedent was alive (which helped him qualify for ALTCS benefits), often times that asset will no longer be exempt after death. The most common asset which loses it exempt status is the decedent's home, which must be used to satisfy any ALTCS lien that arises during the PR's administration.

Phase 3:
Collapsing the Estate

Time to start talking about distributing the estate assets to heirs and beneficiaries. If you are the PR, this is the Phase everyone else is waiting for. Though it might seem simple, doing this part wrong will create liability for the PR and potentially harm family relationships for years to come.

Remember, a typical probate case can last 9-12 months. Heirs are only required to receive information at the start of the probate case and then 90 days later with the inventory. The PR isn't required to send them any further information until the time for distribution. That could be 9 – 12 months later! It is helpful to keep all interested parties aware of what is happening each month of the probate, even if you are simply waiting for a deadline to pass. This will help when it comes time to discuss distributions.

Interim distributions

If the estate has more than enough funds to pay all expenses of administration and all claims (debts), the PR is allowed to make interim distributions at any time. Heirs can be very impatient even if they know of the required waiting periods. With interim distributions, as with all distributions, the risk is the PR discovering that there are more bills to be paid and not enough money left in the estate to pay them. It may be impossible to recover money from an heir.

> ## Problem Spotter:
>
> Don't close before all tax returns have been filed. If you need to re-open the probate, that will cost the estate more.

Final distributions

Final distributions should completely empty the estate of all money and property. Planning out your distributions is best done after everything has been liquidated and deposited into the estate checking account.

Distributions take the following priority:

1. Specific gifts, then

2. Residuary gifts

If there isn't enough money to pay all the gifts, pay only the specific gifts. That would be where someone said in their will "I leave $500 to my nephew, John Smith." If there is more than enough, divide the money and property as fairly and equally as instructed by the will or by the probate court. Remember, the PR will have a very difficult time getting anything back from an heir if there is a mistake. In that case, the PR will be left making up for it out of his or her own pocket.

Time to shut it down

Once there are no funds left in the estate checking, the real estate is sold/ transferred, and the estate owns nothing, prepare a final closing statement.

If a summary closing procedure is available, the PR should prepare a closing statement and file it with the court. Otherwise, the PR has two choices: (1) obtain an order of complete settlement, or (2) file an informal closing statement. If the PR has any question about whether or not an heir will challenge certain actions of distributions, the PR should file a petition for final discharge to obtain an Order of Complete Settlement. This type of closing will result in 100% immediate protection from the court that the PR has completed the job legally. The Order of Complete Settlement will allow all parties to appear at a hearing where the court will determine heirs, probate the Will, and approve the final accounting. If there are any challenges, the court can decide the issues here. The resulting order will discharge the PR of any and all probate concerns.

If the PR does not anticipate any contests, an informal closing can be filed. Once the informal closing statement is filed, any person given notice has six months to challenge the statement. The PR's appointment terminates 12 months after the filing of an informal closing statement.

Final Words

Well that's it. That's as best as I can summarize Arizona's Probate process. When I first wrote this material it was twice as long as it is now, and I already felt like it was leaving out many, many important things. But for a short "guide," I hope you find it helpful.

If you need more help beyond our first meeting, we will discuss the expected fees for that additional work before we wrap it up.

Warm regards,

Francisco P. Sirvent

Attorney & Problem Solver at Law™

If you haven't read Francisco's first book...

Pack Your Parachute: Keeping Peril Out of Your Estate Plan

Read this excerpt here to begin to learn the OTHER perils--aside from probate--that your family can face if your plan is not correctly completed.

Peril #12

Peril #12 is failing to keep your plan current every day.

Think of a time when you stepped up to pay for something with a credit card and immediately learned the card expired? Perhaps you missed the new card in the mail or simply forgot to activate it. It doesn't matter, because the expired card won't buy you even a stick of gum. It's easy to forget to update things. Similarly, even the best-drafted estate plan becomes less relevant over time.

How frequently must you update your estate plan? The truth is no one answer is correct for every person. The best answer is that your estate plan must be perfect the day you die or become incapacitated. If your plan is not perfect, there will likely be unnecessary fees, taxes, costs, and delays waiting just around the corner.

Traditional estate planning works like this: You arrive for a consultation and the attorney charges $3,000-$6,000 for what is known as comprehensive estate planning. This process is different than when you go to a general practice lawyer who pulls a form out, has her secretary fill in the blanks, you sign it, and she collects your check. Comprehensive estate planning goes through many dimensions of getting your affairs in order and gets you fully squared away.

So the attorney then says, "Congratulations! You are now up to date!"

It's a good day.

Have you done a will or trust in the past? And are you 100% confident that your plan will be implemented exactly as you want, paying as little as legally possible in fees, court costs, and taxes if something happened to you right now? When I ask this question in group settings, about half of the group will say they have done a will or trust before. Yet, when I ask how many of those people are 100% confident with their estate plan, all but one or two hands drop. Often, those hands still in the air are already my clients.

Here's the problem. Most traditional estate planning firms ignore the most important fact: you aren't planning to die the day you sign your documents. Most of these firms have no mechanism to keep clients' estate plans current. The reality is estate plans are drafted around all kinds of different laws. In the state of Arizona, there are three major sections of law we must deal with: trust, tax, and probate laws. What's more is we must contend with all the Arizona court opinions interpreting these laws as it pertains to certain specific facts. This set of laws is overlaid on top of another whole set of laws at the federal level, which are also interpreted by federal case decisions.

Monitoring these detailed laws and how they mesh with one another and fit among different variables of each specific situation is critical. This is MY job. It's what I do. You should not have to worry about these changes and laws—your attorney should take that responsibility off your plate.

Some avoid planning their estates because they believe the plan is set in stone and hard to change. Your estate plan, once finished, is not and should not be set in stone.

It should be easy for you to make changes anytime you want. We encourage our clients to make changes as often as they need it. There are a few very rarely used estate-planning techniques that actually are set in stone, but that is not the norm.

No one wants outdated documents in their estate plan. Let's revisit the case I mentioned before regarding my client whose husband is in the conservatorship case. Despite the fact that she had a trust and a power of attorney, the age of these documents concerned their financial institution's compliance department. The financial institution rejected them to protect themselves. After years and dollars spent and many court dates, the financial institution WAS protected. The cost of that protection was my client's dollars—thousands of dollars—my client's time and privacy, and the time and privacy of her husband.

Please don't let this happen to you.

Arizona does not have a law that requires a third party like a bank or financial institution to honor your power of attorney. This is a weakness in Arizona's legal system. Because of this, financial institutions can and often do reject a valid power of attorney.

If you could see an example of a court docket for a conservator case, you would see hundreds of lines with each one representing billable hours. The probate court rules require that attorneys' bill hourly for this work. There's just no way to bill flat fees as an attorney on these cases.

The result is an incredibly expensive bill for anything filed because it must be drafted by one attorney and then read by the other attorney, and then he or she then must generate a response. Then, I must read the response, draft a reply, and so on, and so on.

Having an estate planning attorney that you can trust to keep your plans up-to-date is priceless—in dollars and in peace of mind.

Contact Keystone Law Firm to request your free copy of

Pack Your Parachute: Keeping Peril Out of Your Estate Plan

Call us today at

480-418-1776

Notes:

Notes:

YOUR Arizona Guidebook to Probate